CORRECTIONAL FACILITIES

Zachary A. Kelly

The Rourke Corporation, Inc.
Vero Beach, Florida 32964

© 1999 The Rourke Corporation, Inc.

All rights reserved. No part of this book may be reproduced or utilized in any form or by any means, electronic or mechanical including photocopying, recording, or by any information storage and retrieval system without permission in writing from the publisher.

PHOTO CREDITS:
© California Dept. of Corrections: cover, pages 7, 18, 34; Tony Gray: pages 4, 24, 43, 44; Danny Bachelor: pages 6, 9, 14, 28, 35, 37, 40; © Florida Dept. of Juvenile Justice: pages 5, 12, 16, 21; © Reuters/Jeff Topping/Archive Photos: pages 26; © The Cayuga Museum: pages 30, 31; © Reuters/Dan Levine/Archive Photos: page 41

PRODUCED BY: East Coast Studios, Merritt Island, Florida

EDITORIAL SERVICES:
Penworthy Learning Systems

Library of Congress Cataloging-in-Publication Data

Kelly, Zachary A., 1970-
    Correctional facilities / by Zachary Kelly.
        p. cm. — (Law and order)
    Includes index.
    Summary: Explains the purpose of correctional facilities and describes various kinds including jails and prisons as well as alternatives to incarceration such as probation and parole.
        ISBN 0-86593-578-5
    1. Prisons—United States Juvenile literature. 2. Correctional institutions—United States Juvenile literature. 3. Juvenile corrections—United States Juvenile literature. 4. Jails—United States Juvenile literature. 5. Probation—United States Juvenile literature. [1. Prisons. 2. Corrections 3. Jails. 4. Probation.] I. Title. II. Series.
HV9471.K35   1999
365'.973—dc21   99-28692
                                                                              CIP

Printed in the USA

TABLE OF CONTENTS

Chapter One
PURPOSE OF CORRECTIONS 5

Chapter Two
WHILE IN THE STATE'S CUSTODY 11

Chapter Three
JUVENILE CORRECTION FACILITIES..........17

Chapter Four
JAILS..23

Chapter Five
A BRIEF HISTORY OF PRISONS...................29

Chapter Six
PRISONS..33

Chapter Seven
PROBATION AND PAROLE 39

GLOSSARY 45

FURTHER READING 47

INDEX...48

A person must be arrested and convicted before being sent to a correctional facility.

CHAPTER ONE

PURPOSE OF CORRECTIONS

Every society has ways to punish criminals. Some criminals pay fines. Others work for the community or state without pay. Many criminals go to prison. Punishing criminals is the job of our *corrections system*. The corrections system works with the courts to punish lawbreakers and prevent crimes. The corrections system has four purposes. One is to punish criminals. Another purpose is to help them change. A third purpose is to keep other people from committing crimes. And the fourth purpose is keeping criminals away from the rest of us.

Prison cells are not made to be comfortable. They have metal toilets and beds.

Most criminals go to live in special places called **correctional facilities**. Federal and state prisons are correctional facilities. County jails and juvenile detention centers are correctional facilities also. Criminals who live in correctional facilities are called **inmates**.

Inmates get retribution. Retribution means *something that is deserved*. In other words, a criminal deserves punishment.

Many prisons teach inmates valuable job skills to help with rehabilitation.

Most legal experts give two reasons for punishing criminals. One, punishment is a natural human urge. When somebody does wrong, we naturally wish to punish that person. Two, most people believe punishment is morally right. To be just, though, retribution must fit the crime. By making retribution fit the crime, our corrections system treats inmates fairly.

Inmates get **rehabilitation**. Rehabilitation means helping criminals change so they will not commit more crimes. Inmates go to school, where their teachers and counselors help to rehabilitate them. In school, inmates can learn the skills they need to earn a living. Inmates can get help with their personal problems by talking with counselors. Counselors can help inmates learn to make better choices. When they leave the correctional facilities, inmates take what they learn into everyday life. They can become useful, productive citizens.

Sending criminals to live in correctional facilities is **deterrence**. It works like this: People know that committing a crime will bring about harsh, quick punishment. So they tend not to commit the crime because they fear being punished.

All high-security correctional facilities are surrounded by dangerous fences to prevent escape.

Deterrence can be specific. When a criminal is punished and learns from his or her mistake, deterrence is specific. The person does not want to be punished again, so he or she will not commit the crime again. Deterrence can be general, as when everybody avoids certain crimes because they know strong punishment will follow.

Sending criminals to live in correctional facilities is incapacitation. Inmates are kept away from other people, and they stay in one place. They are maybe told how to spend their time and how to dress. Some prisoners may not choose when or what to eat or how much. Incapacitation is part of their punishment. Incapacitation also protects society from further harm criminals may do.

CHAPTER TWO

WHILE IN THE STATE'S CUSTODY

When criminals go to correctional facilities they are in the state's **custody**. This means the state is responsible for inmates' health and well-being. The U.S. Constitution lets inmates keep many of their rights, but they do not have the same rights as free people. Having fewer rights is part of the punishment. Limiting their rights is also a way to keep inmates orderly and safe. The corrections system works to balance inmates' rights with its goal: retribution, rehabilitation, and incapacitation.

Inmates at a youth detention center are taken outside for exercise.

Rights spelled out in the Constitution are among the most important rights for anyone to keep. The *First Amendment* to the Constitution tells us we have the right to express ourselves freely, gather in groups, and choose our religion. Inmates have these rights, too. In correctional facilities, though, these rights must be limited so they will not interfere with punishment or safety of the inmates. The *Eighth Amendment* gives other important rights to prisoners. It says that inmates cannot be made to take cruel or unusual punishment. What is *cruel*? What is *unusual*? Those questions are hard to answer, but people in our legal system have some answers, and they keep looking for more.

Prisoners must be allowed to keep themselves clean. They cannot be made to live in unsanitary (dirty, unhealthy) conditions. Prisoners must be given enough food and be allowed to exercise regularly. No form of **corporal punishment**, such as beating or whipping, may be used to correct or punish inmates.

All prisoners must have the same right as any other citizen to go to court. Inmates must be allowed to take their complaints before a judge in a court of law.

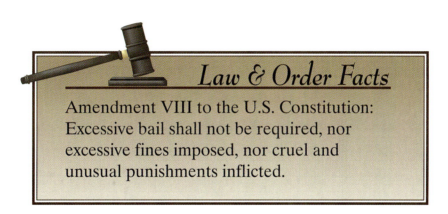

Law & Order Facts
Amendment VIII to the U.S. Constitution: Excessive bail shall not be required, nor excessive fines imposed, nor cruel and unusual punishments inflicted.

An accused person stands before a judge in a courtroom.

Prisoners usually go to court for one of two reasons. One, a prisoner may not agree with his or her sentence and may want to challenge it. This challenge is called an *appeal*. In an appeal, a prisoner uses the right to have his or her case tried again. After looking over the case, the court may change the verdict or leave it as is. Also, prisoners can challenge the conditions of prison life. If a prisoner has a complaint, he or she can bring it before the court. The court will listen to the complaint and decide what, if anything, should be done about it. Along with the right to go to court, prisoners have the right to talk with attorneys and read law books. These rights help them prepare the cases they take to court.

A convicted juvenile looks outside his cell window.

CHAPTER THREE

JUVENILE CORRECTION FACILITIES

Our legal system treats adult and child lawbreakers differently. We have a *dual justice system*. One part of the justice system is for adults and the other is for children. Children aged 8 years to 17 years are called **juveniles**. A person is legally an adult at age 18. Adult criminals usually go to jail or prison, but juveniles may go to some other kinds of correctional facilities. In these facilities, rehabilitation is more important than retribution.

In a secure facility all prisoners are kept behind locked bars.

Juvenile correction facilities may be nonsecure or secure.

Nonsecure facilities have fewer controls than other juvenile facilities. Inmates who live in them live much like the rest of us. Juveniles who commit serious crimes go to secured facilities. Secured facilities set many limits on the inmates, They have strict rules and people to see that rules are followed.

A *shelter* is a short-term nonsecure facility. Juveniles go there for a few days or a week. Some juveniles go to shelters after their arrest, before their trials. Others go to a shelter for a while and then go to a bigger facility.

Law & Order Facts

About 650,000 juvenile arrests take place each year—about 17 out of every 100 arrests.

A *group home* is a nonsecure facility for groups of 4 to 12 juveniles. They usually stay in a group home for several months. Group home inmates go to school. And they often get health care and counseling to help rehabilitate them.

A *halfway house* is a larger nonsecure facility. Usually a halfway house is home for 12 to 20 juveniles. These facilities are set up for rehabilitation. Inmates have to go to school and work and get counseling. At the same time, their way of living is nearly normal.

Other nonsecure facilities include *camps* and *ranches*. These facilities are in the country. Juveniles who go there must work outdoors. The way of life at camps and ranches helps juveniles learn good work habits and self-control.

A *detention center* is a short-term locked (secured) facility. Most detention centers house about 20 juveniles. They often stay there while going through court—usually a week or two. Detention centers keep juveniles locked up for three reasons. One, to make sure the juveniles go to court—instead of running away or becoming a no-show.

Juveniles in a detention center must do what they're told when they're told.

Two, juveniles who commit serious crimes often have terrible home situations. They cannot be allowed to return home. The third reason for locked facilities is to keep inmates from hurting themselves or others.

A *training school* is the most secure corrections facility—for juveniles who commit very serious crimes. Training schools are long-term facilities that hold several hundred inmates. Punishment is as important as rehabilitation in training schools.

CHAPTER FOUR

JAILS

Jails are run by local governments, but prisons are run by state governments or the federal government. In the U.S., counties run about 85 out of 100 jails. Most of the rest are run by city governments. Local jails do three jobs in our legal system. One, jails are where criminal justice starts. When a person is arrested for or questioned about a crime, he or she is taken to the local jail. Two, the local jail holds people waiting for their court appearances. Often the accused cannot pay bail and leave jail. They must wait for a verdict from the court.

RECTOR PUBLIC LIBRARY
121 W. 4th Street
Rector, AR 72461

This type of holding cell is used by local police departments to hold suspects during processing.

Three, jails punish and rehabilitate criminals sentenced to a year or less in a facility.

Three kinds of jails do these jobs. One is a *pretrial detention* facility. This type of jail holds the accused before, during, and immediately after their court appearances. Another kind of jail is called a sentenced facility. These jails hold convicted (proved guilty) criminals. Jail time is usually less than a year, and most inmates are guilty of misdemeanors (minor crimes).

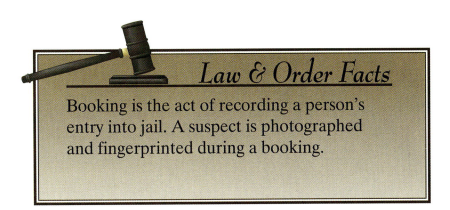

Law & Order Facts

Booking is the act of recording a person's entry into jail. A suspect is photographed and fingerprinted during a booking.

A third kind of jail combines the pretrial detention facility and the sentenced facility. These jails serve many purposes for accused and sentenced people. Going into a local jail involves several steps for an inmate. First, the person is *booked*. This means a record is written about the person and the reason he or she is going to jail. The record includes a picture of the person and his or her fingerprints. Next, the person may be searched, washed, checked by a doctor, and told the jail rules. Leaving jail has fewer steps. When a judge says the inmate can leave, the person only has to walk away.

Most jails are uncomfortable places. Many kinds of people live together in jails. Some inmates are convicted criminals. Others have only been accused, and will be found innocent when they go to court. Some inmates may not be charged at all, but wait to be taken to another facility, like a mental hospital.

A guard stands watch over a few prisoners.

26

Most jails do little to rehabilitate inmates. Jail overcrowding is the main reason. There are too many inmates for each one to get much attention. Also, most inmates stay in jail only a short time. He or she may not be there long enough for rehabilitation to happen. Too little money is another problem for jails that keeps them from rehabilitating inmates. Jails often lack funds for good rehab programs. Many jails don't even have a medical center for inmates. Not many jails have group counseling for them either. Schooling is limited, too. Many inmates cannot get through high school or take college courses. Their short time in jail and the high cost to the state just won't allow it.

Most jails have an administrator like a school's principal.

CHAPTER FIVE

A BRIEF HISTORY OF PRISONS

Prisons have a long history. People have had prisons for thousands of years. Today's prisons go back to the **workhouses** in Europe in the 1500's. A workhouse was a place where criminals and homeless people were sent to do hard work. Before the workhouse, criminals were fined or beaten. The workhouse became popular because people in Europe at that time needed more hard workers. People in a workhouse did lots of jobs: spinning wool, making clothes, baking bread, or mixing mortar for building. People in workhouses were often forced to work long hours in dirty places.

Prisoners in lock-step at the Auburn State Prison in New York.

Around 1750, people began to think of workhouses as places for rehabilitation, not just punishment. Two prison systems grew up in the U.S. One, called the *Pennsylvania system* was begun by Quakers in that state. Quakers were religious people. They believed prisoners could be rehabilitated through religion, hard work, and time alone. In Quaker prisons, the prisoners were kept apart from one another.

1915 work camp

The Quakers built the first American prison, called a **penitentiary**, in 1790. The next prison system, called the *Auburn system*, got its name from the Auburn State Prison in New York, built in 1819. People who started the Auburn system also thought prisoners should be religious and do hard work, but they also thought prisoners should live together in a community. The Auburn system became the one most used in the United States, because community prisons cost less to build.

Early prisons had bad conditions. Inmates were often beaten, starved, or forced to work long hours without rest, or sleep. In 1870, a man named Enoch Wines organized a group, the *World Prison Congress*. This group worked to change the conditions of prison life. By 1900, most people in the U.S. thought that prisons should rehabilitate prisoners, not just punish them. Prisons started to include school and job training for the inmates. Besides being punished, inmates were prepared to earn a living and live a useful life. A hundred years later, most people in the U.S. still think this way.

CHAPTER SIX

PRISONS

We have state prisons and federal prisons. State prisons are for people who break state and local laws. Each state runs these prisons. Federal prisons are for people who break federal laws. The U.S. government runs federal prisons. Criminals sentenced to prison have usually committed felonies (serious crimes). Prison inmates stay longer than people who are sent to jail.

Lunch and recreation rooms must also be kept locked.

The interior of a prison

The average sentence for a violent crime is about three years. About 30 of every 100 prisoners have committed violent crimes. Almost 50 of every 100 have committed some kind of stealing, and 10 out of 100 have committed drug-related crimes. The others have committed several different kinds of crimes. State and federal prisons can be described by how much freedom the inmates have: maximum security (no freedom), medium security (some freedom), minimum security (more freedom). Maximum-security prisons hold criminals who have committed serious crimes.

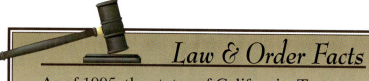

Law & Order Facts

As of 1995, the states of California, Texas, New York, Florida and the Federal system, had the five highest numbers of prison inmates in the country.

These prisons have several goals: keep prisoners from escaping, keep them from hurting themselves or others (like guards), and try to rehabilitate prisoners. Walls 18 to 25 feet high, with barbed wire on top, surround maximum-security prisons. Inmates are housed in long rows of small rooms called *cells*. Usually a group, or *block*, of cells holds hundreds of prisoners. Nearly half of all prisoners are held in maximum-security prisons. A new kind of maximum-security prison is in use now. This kind has 6 to 8 separate units within a walled area. Each unit has its own laundry room, dining room, and common area. The prisoners in a unit all have the same sort of problems. For example, all inmates in one unit may have drug problems, while those in another unit may be violent. This setup lets prisoners interact with others in their unit and still have maximum security.

Hi-tech equipment helps administrators and guards run today's correctional facilities.

37

Medium-security prisons hold criminals who have committed less serious offenses. These prisons are often surrounded by a double fence, instead of a wall. Medium-security facilities focus on rehabilitation. Group-living is the way in most of them. About a third of all prisoners are in these facilities.

Minimum-security prisons hold the least dangerous prisoners. The grounds are often like a school yard, with only a fence around it. Rehabilitation is very important in these prisons, along with living normally in groups. Many minimum-security prisons give prisoners some privacy. Nearly all of these prisons have education programs and counseling. About one in ten prisoners are held in these facilities.

CHAPTER SEVEN

PROBATION AND PAROLE

Holding someone in a jail or prison is called **incarceration**. Other ways to rehab and punish are called **probation** and **parole**. Probation works on the "front end." It is used before a person goes to jail or prison. Local police are usually in charge of probation. Parole works on the "back end." It is used after a person leaves jail or prison. Parole is run by state governments, through the state parole board.

A guard watches as an inmate completes his daily work.

Probation is a sentence, just like a jail sentence, but instead of going to jail, the person lives in the community. He or she has an overseer, a probation officer. After a person is sentenced to jail or prison, the judge may offer probation instead of incarceration. The judge *suspends* the jail sentence and puts a probation sentence in its place. Probation is an agreement between the state and the criminal. The criminal can live outside of jail if he or she obeys certain rules.

These men wait for permission to eat at this rehabilitation facility.

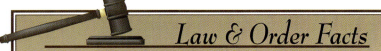

Law & Order Facts

The average maximum prison sentence for murder in the U.S. is about 12 years 5 months. The average time spent in prison for murder is about 5 years 11 months.

    If the rules are ever broken, the person must go to jail immediately. Then he or she must take the judge's first sentence. Probation rules affect where the person works and lives. The rules also affect what kind of restitution, or payback, the criminal can give. The person on probation must go regularly to a **probation officer**. The officer keeps track of the person's progress. The officer can tell if the person is changing in thoughts and actions.

    Parole is not a sentence. Parole is early release from jail or prison. When people are sent to jail, they are told the shortest and longest time they may have to stay. For example, a judge may sentence a violent criminal to at least 2 years but no more than 8 years. State **parole boards** check prisoners about once a year to see if any of them should be released before their maximum (longest) time is up. If the parole board thinks the prisoner can live in society, it will let him or her out on parole.

Breaking probation often means going to jail to serve the sentence.

Once out of jail or prison, the person on parole must obey many rules. For example, someone on parole cannot break any laws. He or she must check in regularly with a parole officer. Anytime he or she breaks these rules, the parole can be taken away. If that happens, the person goes back to jail or prison.

Breaking parole can mean returning to jail.

GLOSSARY

corporal punishment (KAWR pur ul PUN ish munt) — any rough handling of the body done as a penalty

correctional facilities (kuh REK shun ul fuh SIL i teez) — buildings and programs for convicts or those accused of crimes awaiting trial

custody (KUS tuh dee) — held under guard, such as by police; duty of guarding and caring for prisoners

deterrence (deh TER ens) — way of keeping something from happening by having harsh results if it does happen

incarceration (in KAHR suh RAY shun) — state of being held in jail or prison

inmate (IN MAYT) — person held in jail or prison

juveniles (JOO vuh NYLZ) — young people aged 8 to 17 years

parole (Puh ROL) — release of a prisoner whose jail time is not up

parole boards (puh ROL BAWRDZ) — people who decide if and when a convict may be released on parole

GLOSSARY

penitentiary (PEN i TEN shu REE) — prison for major criminals; often refers to the oldest kind of prison

probation (pro BAY shun) — a sentence in place of jail time that involves following certain rules and seeing the officer in charge regularly

probation officer (pro BAY shun AW fi ser) — overseer in charge of people on probation

rehabilitation (REE huh BIL i TAY shun) — to restore useful life, through education, training, and counseling

workhouse (WERK HOUS) — early prison in Europe; sentences required hard work

FURTHER READING

- Brown, Lawrence. *The Supreme Court.* Washington, D.C.: Congressional Quarterly, 1981.
- Conklin, John E. *Criminology.* Allyn and Bacon: Needham Heights, Mass, 1995.
- De Sola, Ralph. *Crime Dictionary.* NY: Facts on File, 1988.
- Hill, Gerald and Hill, Kathleen. *Real Life Dictionary of the Law.* Los Angeles: General Publishing Group, 1995.
- Janosik, Robert ., ed. *Encyclopedia of the American Judicial System.* NY: Charles Scribner and Sons, 1987.
- Johnson, Loch K. *America's Secret Power (CIA).* Oxford: OUP, 1989.
- Kadish, Sanford H., ed. *Encyclopedia of Crime and Justice.* NY: The Free Press, 1983.
- McShane, M. and Williams, F., eds. *Encyclopedia of American Prisons.* NY: Garland, 1996.
- Morris, N. and Rothman, D., eds. *The Oxford History of the Prison.* Oxford: OUP, 1995.
- Regoli, Robert and Hewitt, John. *Criminal Justice.* Prentice-Hall: Englewood Cliffs, NJ, 1996.
- Renstrum, Peter G. *The American Law Dictionary.* Santa Barbara, CA: ABC-CLIO, 1991.
- Territo, Leonard, et al. *Crime & Justice in America.* West: St. Paul, MN, 1995.
- *The Constitution of the United States.* Available in many editions.
- *The Declaration of Independence.* Available in many editions.
- Voigt, Linda, et al. *Criminology and Justice.* McGraw-Hill: New York, 1994.

- http://entp.hud.gov/comcrime.html
  Crime Prevention
  Department of Justice
  PAVNET (Partnership Against Violence Network)
  Justice Information Center
- http://www.fightcrime.com/lcrime.htm
  Safety and Security Connection
  The Ultimate Guide to Safety and Security
  Resources on the Internet
- http://www.internets.com/spolice.htm
  Police Databases
- http://www.psrc.com/lkfederal.html
  Links to most Federal Agencies
- http://www.dare-america.com/
  Official Website of D.A.R.E.

INDEX

appeal   15
attorney   15
booked   25
camps   20
Constitution, The   11, 12
correctional facilities   7, 8, 11
corrections system   5, 8, 11
counselor   8
courts   5
crimes   5, 8
custody   11
cells   36
detention center   20
deterrence   8, 10
dual justice system   17
fingerprints   25
felonies   33
half-way house   20
group home   20
incapacitation   10, 11
incarceration   39, 41
inmates   7, 8, 10, 11, 12, 19, 20, 22, 27, 32, 36

juvenile   17, 19, 20, 22
misdemeanor   24
jails   23, 24, 25, 33, 41, 42, 44
parole   39, 42, 44
   board   42
penitentiary   32
prison   5, 23, 29, 32, 33, 35, 36, 38
   federal   7, 33, 35
   state   7, 33, 35
probation   39, 41, 42
   officer   42, 44
punishment   8, 10, 11, 12, 13, 31,
ranches   20
rehabilitation   8, 11, 20, 27, 31, 38
retribution   7, 11, 17
rights   12
sentence   15, 35, 41
shelter   19
training school   22
verdict   24
workhouse   29, 31

RECTOR PUBLIC LIBRARY
121 W. 4th Street
Rector, AR 72461